LE CORDON BLEU

HOME COLLECTION

QUICHES & SAVORIES

PERIPLUS
EDITIONS

contents

4
Salmon millefeuilles

6
Wild mushroom quiche

8
Gougères

10
Provençal tart

12
Sun-dried tomato twists

14
Spinach and ricotta quiche

16
Leek tartlets

18
Salmon and basil tart

20
Creamy ham tart

22
Three-pepper quiche

24
Shrimp bouchées

26
Potato and bacon tart

28
Sausage rolls

30
Quiche lorraine

32
Cheese palmiers and straws

34
Spinach and Brie tart

36
Fresh crab tartlets

38
Tomato, basil and mozzarella quiche

40
Mussel chaussons with garlic cream

42
Cheese tart

44
Scrambled egg and smoked salmon tartlets

46
Chèvre and watercress quiche

48
Anchovy sticks

50
Leek and Brie flamiche

52
Asparagus feuilletés with chive butter sauce

54
Seafood quiche

56
Ham gougères

58
Chef's techniques

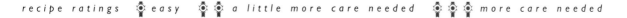

recipe ratings ✦ *easy* ✦✦ *a little more care needed* ✦✦✦ *more care needed*

Salmon millefeuilles

A delicious savory variation of the classic French millefeuille, *this dish is made with layers of flaky puff pastry, lightly cooked salmon and a mouth-watering chive butter sauce.*

Preparation time **1 hour + 15 minutes chilling**
Total cooking time **1 hour 30 minutes**
Serves 4

**1 lb. salmon fillet,
  skin and bones removed**
2 tablespoons olive oil
1/2 quantity puff pastry (see page 60)
1 egg, beaten
4 sprigs fresh chervil or parsley, to garnish

SAUCE
2 shallots, finely chopped
1 cup white wine
1 tablespoon white wine vinegar
1/4 cup heavy cream
3/4 cup unsalted butter, chilled and cubed
3 tablespoons chopped fresh chives

1 Cut the salmon into 24 thin slices, about 1/4-inch thick. Season with salt and pepper, and drizzle with the olive oil. Cover and set aside. Lightly grease a baking sheet and line with waxed paper.
2 Preheat the oven to 425°F. Divide the puff pastry in half, and roll each half out on a lightly floured surface to an 11 1/2 x 10-inch rectangle, 1/8-inch thick. Pierce all over with a fork and refrigerate for 15 minutes. Place one half of the pastry on the baking sheet, and cover with a sheet of waxed paper and a second baking sheet. Bake for 10–15 minutes, then flip the pastry and the baking sheets over and bake for 10 minutes, or until the pastry is light golden and evenly colored. Lightly brush with the beaten egg. Bake, uncovered, for 3–4 minutes, or until glossy. Place on a wire rack to cool slightly, then repeat with the other half of pastry. Cut each sheet of pastry into four 3 1/2-inch squares.
3 To make the sauce, place the shallots in a saucepan with the white wine and vinegar, and bring to a boil over medium heat. Cook until the liquid has almost completely evaporated, about 15–20 minutes. Add the cream and cook for another 2–3 minutes. Whisk in the butter, a few pieces at a time, mixing well after each addition. Season to taste with salt and white pepper.
4 Heat a little olive oil in a skillet over high heat. Cook the salmon slices in batches for about 10 seconds on each side, turning gently. Set aside.
5 Place a square of pastry in the center of each plate. Arrange six slices of salmon on top and cover with a second square of pastry. Whisk the chives into the warm sauce, and drizzle around the base of each millefeuille. Top each with a sprig of chervil, and serve immediately.

Wild mushroom quiche

This quiche may be made with any combination of wild and cultivated mushrooms, depending on what is available. Wild mushrooms have a strong flavor so the proportion of these to the mild-flavored button mushrooms should be adjusted according to personal preference.

*Preparation time **45 minutes***
*Total cooking time **1 hour 10 minutes***
Serves 4–6

¹/2 quantity short pastry (see page 58)
I egg, beaten

FILLING
¹/4 cup unsalted butter
4 cups sliced chanterelles, cèpes (porcini), shiitake,
  oyster, button mushrooms or any
  combination of the above
2 shallots, finely chopped
I egg
2 egg yolks
¹/3 cup heavy cream
I tablespoon each of chopped
  fresh chives, parsley and chervil

1 Lightly grease an 8¹/4 x 1-inch fluted tart pan with removable base. Roll out the pastry on a lightly floured surface to a thickness of ¹/8 inch and line the prepared pan (see Chef's techniques, page 59). Preheat the oven to 350°F. Bake blind for 25 minutes, or until firm. Remove the weights and paper, and brush the bottom of the pastry with the beaten egg. Bake for another 7 minutes (see Chef's techniques, page 59).

2 To make the filling, melt the butter in a nonstick skillet over medium-high heat. Sauté the mushrooms for about 5 minutes, or until all their water has evaporated. (If using more than one type of mushroom, sauté each separately.) Add the chopped shallots and cook for 1 minute, then strain and set aside to cool.

3 Whisk the egg, egg yolks, cream and herbs together. Season to taste with salt and pepper.

4 Spread the mushroom mixture over the bottom of the cooked pastry shell. Pour in the egg mixture, and bake for 25–30 minutes, or until the mixture has set and a knife inserted into the center comes out clean. Place on a wire rack to cool slightly before removing from the pan. Leave for 5 minutes before cutting.

Chef's tip Before using mushrooms, wipe with a damp paper towel; if necessary, rinse with cold water and dry well. Never soak mushrooms as they become mushy.

Gougères

In Burgundy these cheese-flavored puffs are traditionally served cold with wine during tastings in cellars. On page 62 there are step-by-step illustrations to accompany this recipe.

Preparation time **25 minutes**
Total cooking time **25 minutes**
Makes 25–30

¹/₂ cup all-purpose flour
2 tablespoons unsalted butter
pinch of nutmeg
2 eggs
¹/₃ cup finely shredded Gruyère or Cheddar cheese
1 egg, beaten

1 Preheat the oven to 325°F. Lightly grease two baking sheets. Sift the flour onto a sheet of waxed paper. Place ¹/₂ cup water in a saucepan with the butter, nutmeg and a pinch of salt. Heat until the butter and water come to a boil. Remove from the heat and add the flour all at once. Mix well using a wooden spoon. Return to the heat and mix until a smooth ball forms and the paste leaves the sides of the pan. Remove from the heat and place the paste in a bowl. Lightly beat the eggs in a small bowl. Using a wooden spoon or an electric mixer, add the eggs to the paste a little at a time, beating well after each addition. The mixture is ready when it is smooth, thick and glossy. Mix in half the cheese.

2 Spoon the mixture into a pastry bag fitted with a small plain nozzle. Pipe out 1-inch balls of dough onto the prepared sheets, leaving a space of 1¹/4 inches between each ball. Using a fork dipped in the beaten egg, slightly flatten the top of each ball. Sprinkle with the remaining shredded cheese. Bake for 20–25 minutes, or until the balls have puffed up and are golden brown. Serve hot.

Chef's tip This is a very simple and light finger food to serve with pre-dinner drinks. Gougères are sometimes served in restaurants with drinks and referred to as *amuse-gueule*, the French term for appetizer.

Provençal tart

Bursting with the flavors of the south of France, the filling for this yeast-dough tart consists of onion, garlic, tomatoes, zucchini and eggplant, cooked in olive oil and lightly flavored with fresh basil.

*Preparation time **1 hour 15 minutes***
  *+ **40 minutes** proofing*
*Total cooking time **1 hour***
Serves 4–6

PASTRY
1²/3 cups all-purpose flour
1 teaspoon salt
1 teaspoon sugar
1¹/2 teaspoons dry yeast
1 egg
2 tablespoons olive oil

FILLING
olive oil, for cooking
1 small onion, diced
pinch of salt
2 small tomatoes, peeled, seeded and chopped
  (see page 63)
2 cloves garlic, finely chopped
1 zucchini, diced
1 eggplant, diced
1 egg
1 egg yolk
1/3 cup whipping cream
3 tablespoons chopped fresh basil

1 To make the pastry, sift together the flour, salt and sugar into a large bowl. Make a well in the center. In a bowl, dissolve the yeast in 1/4 cup warm water. Whisk in the egg and olive oil, pour into the well and gradually mix in the flour mixture using a wooden spoon. Once a rough dough has formed, turn it out onto a floured work surface, scraping the bowl out if necessary. Knead the dough for about 5 minutes, or until it is smooth and it no longer sticks to the surface. Lightly brush a bowl with oil and place the dough inside. Cover with an oiled piece of plastic wrap and set aside to rise in a warm place for about 30–40 minutes, or until it is doubled in volume.

2 To make the filling, heat a little olive oil in a deep skillet. Add the onion and salt, and cook over medium heat for 3–5 minutes, or until soft, without browning the onion. Add the tomatoes and garlic, and continue to cook over low heat, stirring occasionally, for about 3 minutes, or until the liquid evaporates. Sauté the zucchini and eggplant separately in some olive oil. Add to the tomato mixture, cover and cook over low heat for 15 minutes. Season to taste with salt and pepper, and transfer to a bowl set in ice. Allow to cool, stirring from time to time.

3 Preheat the oven to 325°F. Lightly grease an 8¹/4 x 1-inch fluted tart pan with removable base. Whisk together the egg, egg yolk and cream in a small bowl. Season with salt and pepper.

4 Punch the dough down and turn out onto a floured work surface. Lightly dust with flour, roll out to a 1/8-inch thickness and line the prepared pan (see Chef's techniques, page 59). Cover with a clean damp towel and set aside.

5 Mix the egg mixture and chopped basil into the cool vegetables. Pour into the pastry shell and bake for 30–35 minutes, or until the pastry is nicely colored. Place on a wire rack to cool slightly before removing from the pan. Leave for 5 minutes before cutting.

Sun-dried tomato twists

These light, tomato-flavored twists are excellent served either cold or warm. Perfect to serve with drinks, they may be prepared well in advance and stored in an airtight container.

Preparation time **20 minutes**
 + 1 hour 15 minutes chilling
Total cooking time **15 minutes**
Makes about 80

2 cups all-purpose flour
1/2 teaspoon salt
pinch of pepper
pinch of paprika
1/2 teaspoon baking powder
2/3 cup unsalted butter, chilled and cubed
dash of Tabasco
1/3 cup chopped fresh chives
I egg, lightly beaten
1/3 cup tomato paste
1/3 cup finely chopped sun-dried tomatoes

1 Grease two baking sheets. Sift the flour into a bowl with the salt, pepper, paprika and baking powder. Add the butter and Tabasco, and rub into the flour with your fingertips until the mixture resembles fine bread crumbs. Stir in the chives and make a well in the center.

2 Lightly whisk the egg in a small bowl, pour half into a bowl with half of the tomato paste, and discard the remaining egg. Using a flat-bladed knife, stir into the flour mixture in a circular motion until combined. Gather together into a rough ball of dough. Wrap in plastic wrap and refrigerate for 1 hour.

3 Roll out the dough on a lightly floured surface to a thickness of 1/8 inch. Place on a clean baking sheet, cover with plastic wrap and refrigerate for 15 minutes.

4 Preheat the oven to 400°F. Place the remaining tomato paste and the sun-dried tomatoes in a food processor or blender, and process to a smooth paste. Spread over the pastry, cut into 1/2-inch-wide strips and twist evenly.

5 Place the twists on the prepared baking sheets, giving each one a twist as you place it on the sheet. Press the ends onto the sheet to prevent them from unwinding. Bake for 10–15 minutes, or until golden brown and firm to the touch. Cut the twists into 23/4-inch lengths while still hot. Transfer to a wire rack to cool before serving.

Spinach and ricotta quiche

The classic combination of spinach and ricotta cheese, subtly enhanced with the flavor
of nutmeg, makes a delicious filling for this vegetarian quiche.

*Preparation time **30 minutes***
*Total cooking time **1 hour 10 minutes***
Serves 4–6

FILLING
1 lb. young spinach
1 tablespoon unsalted butter
3 eggs
3/4 cup ricotta cheese
1/3 cup heavy cream
nutmeg, to taste

1/2 quantity short pastry (see page 58)
1 egg, beaten

1 To make the filling, wash the spinach well, remove the stems and pat dry with paper towels. Melt the butter in a deep skillet over medium heat. Add the spinach and cook for about 8 minutes, or until it is wilted and the water has evaporated. Place in a strainer to cool, squeeze out any excess liquid and then finely chop the spinach.

2 Preheat the oven to 350°F. Lightly grease an 81/4 x 1-inch fluted tart pan with removable base. Roll out the pastry on a lightly floured surface to a thickness of 1/8 inch and line the prepared pan (see Chef's techniques, page 59). Bake blind for about 25 minutes, or until firm. Remove the weights and paper, and brush the bottom of the pastry with the beaten egg. Bake for another 7 minutes (see Chef's techniques, page 59).

3 Whisk the eggs, cheese and cream in a bowl, and add the spinach. Season with salt, pepper and nutmeg. Pour into the pastry shell and bake for 25–30 minutes, or until set and a knife inserted into the center comes out clean. Place on a wire rack to cool slightly before removing from the pan. Allow to stand for 5 minutes before cutting.

Leek tartlets

These small tartlets filled with leek and cumin are ideal served warm with drinks. Alternatively, they could be made as larger tarts and served as a first course.

Preparation time **45 minutes + 15 minutes chilling**
Total cooking time **40 minutes**
Makes 30

FILLING
3 tablespoons unsalted butter
I large leek, white part only, thinly sliced
(see page 63)
I bay leaf
pinch of dried thyme
pinch of salt
1/4 teaspoon ground cumin
2/3 cup heavy cream
I egg
I egg yolk

I quantity short pastry (see page 58)

1 To make the filling, melt the butter in a saucepan over low heat. Add the leek, bay leaf, thyme and salt.

Cover and cook slowly for 5 minutes, then uncover and continue cooking for about 5–10 minutes, or until the mixture is dry. Remove the bay leaf. Add the cumin, mix well and set aside to cool.

2 Grease three 12-cup mini muffin pans or gem pans. Roll out the pastry on a lightly floured surface to a thickness of 1/8 inch and refrigerate for 5 minutes. Preheat the oven to 325°F. Using a 23/4-inch plain round cutter, cut out 30 rounds from the pastry. Press the rounds into the prepared muffin pans or gem pans, pressing well along the bottoms so the dough extends slightly above the edge of the pans. Refrigerate the lined pans for 10 minutes.

3 Whisk together the cream, egg and egg yolk, and season with salt and freshly ground black pepper. Fill each pastry shell with 1/2 teaspoon of the leek mixture, then carefully pour in the cream mixture. Bake for 10–15 minutes, or until the filling is set. Remove the tartlets from the pans while they are still warm. If they stick, loosen the tartlets carefully with the tip of a small, sharp knife.

Salmon and basil tart

A delicately flavored tart, excellent served as a light lunch on a hot summer's day with a crisp green salad and a glass of chilled dry white wine.

Preparation time **40 minutes**
Total cooking time **1 hour**
Serves 4–6

1/2 quantity short pastry (see page 58)
1 egg, beaten

FILLING
10 oz. fresh salmon, skin and bones removed
1 egg
2/3 cup heavy cream
3/4 cup milk
1 tablespoon finely chopped fresh basil

1 Preheat the oven to 350°F. Lightly grease an 8³/4 x 1-inch fluted tart pan with removable base. Roll out the pastry on a lightly floured surface to a thickness of 1/8 inch and line the prepared pan (see Chef's techniques, page 59). Bake blind for about 25 minutes, or until firm. Remove the weights and paper, and brush the bottom of the pastry with the beaten egg. Bake for another 7 minutes (see Chef's techniques, page 59).

2 To make the filling, cut the salmon into small cubes. Place in a food processor and process in short bursts until finely chopped. Add the egg and process for 10 seconds, then add the cream and process until smooth. Transfer to a mixing bowl and whisk in the milk. Season to taste with salt and pepper and stir in the basil.

3 Pour the mixture into the pastry shell, and bake for 20–30 minutes, or until the filling is set. The tip of a knife inserted into the center should come out clean. Place on a wire rack to cool slightly before removing from the pan. Allow the tart to cool slightly before serving. Serve warm with a green salad.

Chef's tip For added texture and flavor, crumbled pieces of poached salmon or chopped smoked salmon may be sprinkled over the bottom before the tart is filled.

Creamy ham tart

*Slices of ham in a creamy white sauce, topped with golden-brown melted cheese make this a
popular tart with adults and children alike. A variation of this recipe could be made by using
smoked ham or by adding a little Dijon mustard to the sauce.*

Preparation time **30 minutes + 20 minutes cooling**
Total cooking time **45 minutes**
Serves 4–6

**¹/2 quantity short pastry
  (see page 58)**

FILLING
¹/4 cup unsalted butter
¹/2 cup all-purpose flour
2 cups milk
**5 oz. ham, cut into
  1¹/2 x ¹/2-inch strips**
pinch of nutmeg
**²/3 cup shredded or thinly sliced
  Emmenthal or Gruyère cheese**

1 Preheat the oven to 350°F. Grease a 7¹/4 x 1-inch
fluted tart pan with removable base. Roll out the pastry
on a lightly floured surface to a circle approximately
¹/8–¹/4-inch thick, and line the prepared pan (see Chef's
techniques, page 59).

2 Bake blind for 10 minutes, or until firm. Remove the

weights and paper, and bake for another 5 minutes, or
until the center begins to color (see Chef's techniques,
page 59). Remove from the oven to cool and reduce the
temperature to 325°F.

3 To make the filling, melt the butter in a heavy-
bottomed saucepan over medium heat. Sprinkle the
flour over the base of the pan and cook for 1–2 minutes
without coloring, stirring constantly with a wooden
spoon. Gradually add the milk to the flour mixture,
whisking vigorously to avoid lumps. Be careful not to
splash the milk. Stir constantly over medium heat,
bubbling, for about 8 minutes, or until the sauce is thick
and creamy and is reduced by about two-thirds. When a
spoon is drawn across the base of the pan, the base
should be clearly seen. Stir in the ham and nutmeg, and
season with salt and pepper. Cover the surface with
waxed paper, and set aside to cool for 20 minutes.

4 Spread the mixture into the pastry shell. Sprinkle the
cheese on top and bake for about 10–15 minutes, or
until the cheese is golden and bubbling. For added color,
finish the tart by placing it under a hot broiler for about
30 seconds. Place on a wire rack to cool slightly before
removing from the pan. Leave for 15–20 minutes to set
before cutting into wedges. Serve warm.

Three-pepper quiche

Both colorful and tasty, this quiche is best served warm. If yellow bell peppers are not available, use red and green only, bearing in mind that the red pepper has a much softer, sweeter flavor than the green.

Preparation time **45 minutes**
Total cooking time **1 hour 35 minutes**
Serves **4–6**

FILLING
1 red bell pepper
1 yellow bell pepper
1 green bell pepper
3 eggs
1 cup heavy cream
nutmeg, to taste
1/3 cup shredded Gruyère cheese

1/2 quantity short pastry (see page 58)
1 egg, beaten

1 To make the filling, broil the peppers following the method in the Chef's techniques on page 63, then slice the flesh lengthwise into strips.

2 Preheat the oven to 325°F. Lightly grease an 8 3/4 x 1 1/4-inch fluted tart pan with removable base. Roll out the pastry on a lightly floured surface to a thickness of 1/8 inch and line the prepared pan (see Chef's techniques, page 59). Bake blind for about 25 minutes, or until firm. Remove the weights and paper, and brush the bottom of the pastry with the beaten egg. Bake for another 7 minutes (see Chef's techniques, page 59).

3 Whisk together the eggs and cream, and season to taste with salt, freshly ground black pepper and nutmeg. Spread the peppers over the bottom of the cooked pastry shell and then sprinkle with the shredded cheese. Pour in the egg mixture and bake for 40 minutes, or until the mixture has set and a knife inserted into the center comes out clean. Place on a wire rack to cool slightly before removing from the pan. Allow the quiche to set for 5 minutes before cutting and serving warm Serve the quiche with a crisp green salad.

Shrimp bouchées

Bouchées are small round shells of puff pastry with a tasty filling. These were fashionable at the court of Louis XV of France and his wife, renowned for her hearty appetite.

*Preparation time **15 minutes + 35 minutes chilling***
*Total cooking time **20 minutes***
*Makes **8***

1/2 quantity puff pastry (see page 60)
I egg, beaten

FILLING
2 tablespoons unsalted butter
1/4 cup all-purpose flour
I cup fish or shellfish stock, or milk
1/2 lb. cooked shelled shrimp
2 tablespoons chopped mixed fresh herbs

1 Brush a large baking sheet with butter, and refrigerate until needed. Roll out the pastry on a lightly floured surface to a 1/4-inch thickness. Brush off any excess flour from the surface and cut out eight circles with a 2 3/4-inch fluted round cutter. Sprinkle the prepared sheet with a little cold water, turn the circles over and place on the sheet. Brush with the egg, chill for 5 minutes, then brush again. Using a floured 2-inch plain round cutter, press into the pastry three-quarters of the way through to mark an inner circle. Refrigerate for 30 minutes.

2 Preheat the oven to 425°F. Brush the top of each pastry circle again with beaten egg. Bake on the middle shelf of the oven for 10–12 minutes, or until the pastry circles are well risen, crisp and golden. Remove from the oven and cut around the center circle to remove the lid while still warm. Scrape out the excess soft pastry from inside the little shells. If you wish, return to the oven for 30 seconds to dry. (You may turn the oven off and use its residual heat to do this.)

3 To make the filling, melt the butter in a saucepan, add the flour and cook over low heat for 1 minute. Remove from the heat and pour in the stock or milk, blend thoroughly with a wooden spoon and return to the stove. Stir constantly over low heat until the mixture is free of lumps. Increase the heat and stir until the mixture boils, then simmer for 2–3 minutes. Just before serving, stir in the shrimp to warm through. Finally add the herbs and season to taste with salt and freshly ground black pepper.

4 Spoon the filling into the pastry shells while both are still warm. If you wish, garnish with chopped herbs or extra shrimp. You may replace the lid or not.

Chef's tips If using frozen cooked shrimp, they must be well thawed and drained. Do not wash them, or thaw in cold water, as they will lose a lot of flavor.

After cutting out the pastry circles, they are turned over on the baking sheet to help them to rise with straight sides.

If the cooked shells are left to cool, reheat in a 350°F oven for 5 minutes and fill with the hot filling.

Potato and bacon tart

This delicious tart is made of short pastry topped with thinly sliced potatoes, bacon, cheese, parsley and a creamy filling, and is best served warm. It is important to slice the potatoes thinly to make sure that they cook completely.

*Preparation time **25 minutes***
*Total cooking time **1 hour***
Serves 6

1/2 quantity short pastry (see page 58)

FILLING
1 potato, thinly sliced
4 slices bacon, cut into 1/2-inch-wide strips
2 eggs
1/2 cup heavy cream
1/3 cup milk
1 teaspoon finely chopped fresh parsley
1/2 cup shredded Emmenthal or Gruyère cheese

1 Preheat the oven to 350°F. Grease a 10³/4 x 7¹/2 x 1-inch rectangular tart pan with a removable base. Roll out the pastry on a floured surface approximately 1/8-inch thick and line the prepared pan (see Chef's techniques, page 59).

2 Bake blind for 10 minutes, or until firm. Remove the weights and paper, and bake for another 5 minutes, or until the center begins to color (see Chef's techniques, page 59). Remove from the oven to cool and reduce the temperature to 325°F.

3 To make the filling, pat the potato slices dry with paper towels. Put the bacon in a small saucepan, cover with cold water, bring to a boil and cook for 2 minutes, then drain. Mix the eggs, cream and milk together in a small bowl, and season with salt and pepper.

4 Arrange the potato slices and bacon evenly on the bottom of the pastry shell, and sprinkle the parsley and cheese over the top. Pour in the egg mixture and bake for 35–45 minutes, or until the tart is set, the surface is golden and bubbly, and the potatoes are cooked. (Test by inserting the tip of a knife to check that the potatoes are tender.) Place on a wire rack to cool slightly before removing from the pan. Serve the tart warm with a crisp green salad.

Sausage rolls

Versatile, crisp, golden puff pastry filled with well-seasoned fresh bulk sausage. Sausage rolls are a light luncheon or picnic dish with salad or a lunchbox standby. Mini sausage rolls would make elegant cocktail savories for special occasions.

Preparation time **15 minutes + 15 minutes chilling**
Total cooking time **25 minutes**
Makes 8

I tablespoon unsalted butter
2 shallots, finely chopped
1/2 lb. fresh bulk pork sausage
pinch of ground cinnamon
pinch of ground nutmeg
I tablespoon finely chopped fresh parsley
I quantity puff pastry (see page 60)
I egg, beaten with a pinch of salt

1 Melt the butter in a skillet and add the shallots. Cover and cook over moderate heat for 5 minutes, or until softened. Remove from the pan and allow to cool for 5 minutes. Put the sausage in a bowl and add the shallots, cinnamon, nutmeg and parsley. Season with salt and pepper, and mix well. Roll the sausage mixture out with well-floured palms on a well-floured surface to a long rope 1-inch thick. Transfer to a lightly floured baking sheet and chill while preparing the pastry.

2 Roll the pastry on a lightly floured surface to a long rectangle 1/8-inch thick and at least 4 inches wide. Trim the edges to neaten. Lay the rope of sausage down the length of the pastry just off center, and trim off the excess pastry at the two ends. Brush the smaller width of visible pastry next to the sausage rope with beaten egg, and fold the larger piece of pastry over the sausage to enclose it. Lightly press together the two pastry edges to seal. Trim the edges to neaten. With a lightly floured, thin sharp knife, cut into eight individual sausage rolls. Make three diagonal slits on top of each roll through to the meat to decorate, but also to allow the excess steam to escape. Place on a baking sheet that has been lightly dampened with cold water. Brush with beaten egg, avoiding the open cut edges or they will seal during baking and prevent the pastry from rising. Refrigerate for 15 minutes.

3 Preheat the oven to 425°F. Brush the pastry again with the beaten egg and bake in the top half of the oven for about 25 minutes, or until well risen, crisp and golden brown. Serve hot or cold.

Chef's tips You can easily make mini sausage rolls for serving with cocktails or try interesting variations to the filling by adding herbs or chopped sun-dried tomatoes to the sausage.

For another simple variation, hard-cook and shell quail eggs. Flatten the sausage rope and arrange the eggs in a line down the center. Fold and shape the sausage around them.

The bases of these sausage rolls will be dark brown.

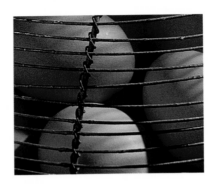

Quiche lorraine

This open tart originated in the Lorraine region around the sixteenth century. The name quiche comes from the German word küchen, *meaning cake. A quiche can contain many fillings, but a quiche lorraine is traditionally made with cream, eggs and smoked bacon, and is considered a classic of French cuisine.*

*Preparation time **30 minutes***
*Total cooking time **1 hour 5 minutes***
Serves 4–6

1/2 quantity short pastry
(see page 58)
1 egg, beaten

FILLING
oil, for cooking
6 oz. slab bacon, rind removed
and cut into thin strips
3 eggs
nutmeg, to taste
1 cup whipping cream
2/3 cup shredded Gruyère cheese

1 Lightly grease an 83/4 x 11/4-inch fluted tart pan with removable base. Roll out the dough on a lightly floured surface to a thickness of 1/8 inch and line the prepared pan (see Chef's techniques, page 59). Preheat the oven to 350°F. Bake blind for about 25 minutes, or until firm. Remove the weights and paper, and brush the bottom of the pastry with the beaten egg. Bake for another 7 minutes (see Chef's techniques, page 59).
2 To make the filling, heat a little oil in a skillet. Sauté the bacon, drain on paper towels and set aside. Whisk the eggs with the nutmeg, and season with salt and freshly ground black pepper. Mix in the cream and strain through a sieve.
3 Sprinkle the bottom of the pastry with the bacon and cheese. Gently pour in the egg mixture until the pastry is three-quarters full. Bake for about 20–30 minutes, or until the filling is well colored and is set. Serve hot.

Cheese palmiers and straws

These small savories are delicious served with a cocktail or to accompany a soup. They can either be made as palmiers or as cheese straws, and flavored with herbs, sun-dried tomatoes or anchovies.

Preparation time **30 minutes + 45 minutes chilling**
Total cooking time **10 minutes**
Makes 30 palmiers or 45 cheese straws

2 egg yolks
I egg
1/4 teaspoon sugar
1/3 cup grated Parmesan
1/4 teaspoon paprika
I quantity puff pastry (see page 60)

1   Beat together the egg yolks, egg, sugar and 1/4 teaspoon salt, and strain into a clean bowl.
2   Grease a large baking sheet with melted butter, and refrigerate until needed. In a small bowl, mix together the Parmesan, paprika and 1/4 teaspoon salt, and season with freshly ground black pepper.
3   Roll out the pastry on a lightly floured surface to a 91/2 x 8-inch rectangle, 1/8 inch thick. Brush lightly with the egg mixture and sprinkle evenly with the Parmesan mixture. Roll again to a 1/8-inch thickness to press the cheese into the pastry. Carefully slide the pastry onto a clean baking sheet and refrigerate for 15 minutes. Transfer the pastry to a lightly floured surface and trim to a 12 x 6-inch rectangle.
4   To make the cheese palmiers, lightly mark six 2-inch-wide strips with the back of a knife, parallel with the shortest side. Do not cut, only mark as a guide. Sprinkle lightly with water.
5   Fold the two outer strips inwards to lay flat. Their non-cheese undersides will now be on top—brush them with a little water and fold over onto the next marked sixths, brush again and fold onto each other to make a stack. Transfer to a clean baking sheet and refrigerate for 15 minutes. Cut into 1/4-inch slices and place cut-side-down, well apart, on the greased baking sheet. Press them down lightly with the palm of your hand to flatten them, turn them over and refrigerate for 15 minutes.
6   Meanwhile, preheat the oven to 400°F. Bake the palmiers for about 10 minutes, or until golden and crisp. Immediately remove from the baking sheet onto a wire rack to cool.
7   To make the cheese straws, follow steps 1–3. Using a large sharp knife, cut the pastry lengthwise into 1/2-inch-wide strips and twist each strip several times to form one long, even, loose ringlet. Place on a baking sheet and press both ends down firmly to stop the strip from unraveling as it bakes. Refrigerate for 10–15 minutes. Meanwhile, preheat the oven to 400°F. Bake for 7–10 minutes, or until golden brown and crisp. Immediately cut each straw into 4-inch lengths and transfer to a wire rack to cool.

Chef's tip Add some dried mixed herbs to the cheese, or some finely chopped sun-dried tomatoes or anchovies.

Spinach and Brie tart

Creamy Brie cheese is combined with onions, spinach and tomatoes for the filling of this puff-pastry tart. It is best served warm with a tomato or crisp green salad.

*Preparation time **25 minutes***
*Total cooking time **1 hour***
Serves 6

1/2 quantity puff pastry (see page 60)
1 egg, beaten

FILLING
2 tablespoons unsalted butter
1 onion, chopped
3 large scallions, cut into thin
  3/4-inch sticks
1 cup frozen spinach, thawed
1 egg
3/4 cup heavy cream
8 oz. Brie, thinly sliced
2 ripe tomatoes, thinly sliced and dried
  on paper towels
2 tablespoons grated Parmesan

1 Lightly grease a 71/4 x 1-inch fluted tart pan with removable base. Preheat the oven to 400°F. Roll out the pastry on a lightly floured surface to 1/16-inch thick, or as thinly as you can—thin enough to read through it— and line the prepared pan (see Chef's techniques, page 59).

2 Bake blind for 15–20 minutes, or until golden. Remove the weights and paper, return to the oven for 5 minutes, then brush the pastry shell with the beaten egg (see Chef's techniques, page 59). Reduce the oven to 350°F.

3 To make the filling, melt the butter in a skillet. Add the onion and cook for about 3 minutes, or until soft. Add the scallions, cook for 1 minute, then add the spinach. Season generously with salt and pepper, and stir until well mixed. Cook over high heat for about 7 minutes, or until the liquid has evaporated.

4 Whisk the egg and cream together in a bowl, and season with salt and pepper. Place the spinach mixture on the bottom of the pastry, cover with a layer of Brie slices and lay the tomatoes evenly on top. Pour the egg and cream mixture over the tomatoes and sprinkle the Parmesan over the top. Bake for about 25 minutes, or until set and golden. Place on a wire rack to cool slightly before removing from the pan. Serve the tart warm.

Fresh crab tartlets

These tartlets may be made to any size, depending on whether they are to be served as finger food, a first course, or as part of a buffet lunch or supper. The pastry shells, however, should not be filled too far in advance or the pastry will become soggy.

Preparation time **2 hours + 15 minutes chilling**
Total cooking time **15 minutes**
Makes 8

FILLING
1 cucumber
1/2 teaspoon salt
1 yellow bell pepper
2 tomatoes, peeled and seeded (see page 63)

1/2 quantity short pastry (see page 58)
1/2 lb. fresh crab meat
2 tablespoons chopped fresh chives

MAYONNAISE
1 egg yolk
2 teaspoons Dijon mustard
1/2 cup oil

1 To make the filling, cut the ends from the cucumber and peel. Cut in half lengthwise and scrape out the seeds using a teaspoon. Cut into very small dice, about 1/8 inch. Toss with the salt. Trim the bell pepper, remove the seeds, and dice the same size as the cucumber. Cut the tomatoes into dice the same size as the cucumber and pepper, and drain on paper towels.

2 Preheat the oven to 325°F. Grease eight 2 3/4 x 5/8-inch fluted tartlet pans. Roll out the pastry on a lightly floured surface to a thickness of 1/8 inch. Refrigerate for 5 minutes. Using a 4-inch round cutter, cut out eight rounds. Ease a pastry round into each pan,

pressing well along the bottoms so that the dough extends slightly above the edges of the pans. Refrigerate for 10 minutes.

3 Trim the pastry to fit the pans. Lightly pierce the base of the pastry with a fork, and bake blind for 8–10 minutes, or until the pastry colors slightly. Remove the weights and paper, and bake for another 2–3 minutes, or until golden brown (see Chef's techniques, page 59). Cool the tartlets for 5 minutes before removing from the pans and placing on a wire rack to cool.

4 To make the mayonnaise, whisk the egg yolk and mustard in a deep bowl until smooth. Gradually whisk in the oil in a steady stream. Once all the oil has been incorporated, season to taste with salt and ground white pepper. Mix 3–4 tablespoons of the mayonnaise into the crab until the mixture holds together. Set aside.

5 Strain off the excess water from the cucumbers, then drain on paper towels and pat dry. Place all the diced vegetables in a bowl and mix in 2–3 tablespoons of the mayonnaise until the mixture holds together. Divide the filling among the tartlet shells, then top with the crab. Spoon a little mayonnaise on top of each tart, and sprinkle with the chopped chives.

Chef's tips Each step can be prepared in advance but do not fill the tartlet shells until ready to serve. For a different flavor, mix a little curry powder into the vegetable mixture.

If using frozen or canned crab meat, remove excess water by placing in a clean towel or cheesecloth and squeezing out all the liquid.

Tomato, basil and mozzarella quiche

A quiche with an Italian twist of flavors that is excellent served either warm or cold,
making it ideal for picnics or lunch boxes.

*Preparation time **30 minutes***
*Total cooking time **1 hour 10 minutes***
Serves 6

1/2 quantity short pastry
  (see page 58)

FILLING
2 eggs
3 tablespoons milk
1/4 cup heavy cream
pinch of nutmeg, optional
pinch of cayenne, optional
2 small tomatoes, halved, seeded and cut into
  1/2-inch pieces
1 cup shredded mozzarella cheese
1 tablespoon finely chopped fresh basil
  (see Chef's tip)

1 Preheat the oven to 400°F. Grease an 8¹/4 x 1-inch fluted tart pan with removable base. Roll out the pastry on a lightly floured surface to a ¹/8-inch thick and line the prepared pan (see Chef's techniques, page 59).

2 Bake blind for 10–15 minutes, or until firm. Remove the weights and paper, and bake for another 10 minutes, or until dry and golden (see Chef's techniques, page 59). Remove from the oven to cool. Reduce the temperature of the oven to 325°F.

3 To make the filling, beat together the eggs, milk and cream in a bowl. Season with salt and pepper, adding the nutmeg and cayenne to taste, if using. Sprinkle the tomatoes, cheese and basil over the base of the tart shell. Pour in the egg mixture and bake for 35–45 minutes. Check from time to time to make sure that the filling is not bubbling. If it is bubbling, the oven is too hot and the temperature should be lowered. When cooked, the filling should be just firm to the touch and the surface golden brown. Place on a wire rack to cool slightly before removing from the pan. Serve warm or cold, accompanied by a crisp green salad.

Chef's tip The basil should be chopped just before using to prevent it from discoloring.

Mussel chaussons with garlic cream

A chausson, literally meaning slipper in French, is a pastry turnover, or semicircular shape, made from a thin round of puff pastry folded over a filling. These are best served warm.

*Preparation time **1 hour 10 minutes**
    + 25 minutes chilling*
*Total cooking time **50 minutes***
Serves 4

1/2 quantity puff pastry (see page 60)
I egg, beaten with a pinch of salt
3 sprigs fresh chervil, to garnish

FILLING
2 tablespoons unsalted butter
I carrot, cut into julienne strips (see Chef's tip)
I small leek, white part only, cut into julienne strips
    (see page 63)
I stalk celery, cut into julienne strips
few drops of lemon juice
1/3 cup dry white wine
2 shallots, finely chopped
2 lb. fresh mussels, scrubbed and beards removed

GARLIC CREAM
10 cloves garlic
1 1/4 cups heavy cream

1 Roll out the pastry on a lightly floured surface to 1/8-inch thick. Cut out eight circles with a 5-inch plain round cutter. Place on a baking sheet and refrigerate for at least 10 minutes. Lightly grease a baking sheet with melted butter and chill until needed.

2 To make the filling, melt the butter in a shallow skillet and add the carrot, leek and celery. Season lightly with salt and pepper. Cover and cook over low heat for 6–10 minutes, or until soft and transparent. Add lemon juice to taste, and cool.

3 Put the wine and shallots in a saucepan or kettle and add the mussels, checking to make sure they are closed.

Discard any that remain open as you handle them. Cover the pan, bring to a boil and simmer for about 5 minutes, or until all the mussels have opened. Discard any that have not opened. Drain and reserve the liquid. Reserve eight mussels in their shells. Remove the remaining mussels from their shells and allow to cool.

4 Place the pastry on a lightly floured surface. Brush a 1/2-inch border of beaten egg around the top edge of each circle. Cover half of each circle, within the limit of the egg, with the vegetables and shelled mussels. Turn the unfilled side over to form a semicircle and press the edges with the back of a fork to seal. Make two small cuts on the top with the point of a small sharp knife to allow the steam to escape during baking. Use the knife point to score pattern marks, crisscross or pinwheel, but do not cut through the pastry. Sprinkle a few drops of water on the greased baking sheet and place the turnovers on the sheet. Brush their surface, but not the cut edges, with the beaten egg, and refrigerate for 15 minutes. Preheat the oven to 425°F. Brush again with beaten egg. Bake for 5 minutes, then reduce the heat to 400°F and bake for 10–15 minutes, or until the turnovers are well risen, crisp and golden brown.

5 To make the garlic cream, put the garlic in a small saucepan, cover with cold water and bring to a boil. Drain and repeat once more. Return the garlic to the pan, add the cream and 1/3 cup of the strained mussel cooking liquid, cover and simmer gently for 15 minutes, or until the garlic is soft. Pour into a blender or food processor, and process until smooth. Season with salt and pepper.

6 To serve, spoon the hot garlic cream over the base of four warm plates, set the hot turnovers on top and garnish with the reserved mussels and sprigs of chervil.

Chef's tip Julienne strips are even-size strips of vegetables, the size and shape of matchsticks.

Cheese tart

The Dijon mustard added to this delicious rich tart filling gives the cheese flavor a good lift.
If desired, a small amount of cayenne pepper could also be added.

*Preparation time **20 minutes***
*Total cooking time **50 minutes***
Serves 6

¹/₂ quantity short pastry (see page 58)

FILLING
1¹/₄ cups shredded Gruyère cheese
3 eggs
³/₄ cup heavy cream
pinch of nutmeg
¹/₄ teaspoon Dijon mustard

1 Preheat the oven to 350°F. Grease an 8¹/₄ x 1-inch fluted tart pan with removable base. Roll out the short pastry on a lightly floured surface to a circle about ¹/₈-inch thick and line the prepared pan (see Chef's techniques, page 59).

2 Bake blind for 10 minutes, or until firm. Remove the weights and paper, and bake for another 5–10 minutes, or until the center begins to color (see Chef's techniques, page 59). Remove from the oven to cool.

3 Sprinkle the cheese over the base of the pastry. Whisk together the eggs, cream, nutmeg and mustard, and season with salt and pepper. Pour the mixture over the cheese and bake for 20–30 minutes, or until the mixture is set and golden brown. Place on a wire rack to cool slightly before removing from the pan.

4 You can serve the tart either warm or cold with a fresh green salad and tomatoes for a refreshing, light summer lunch.

Scrambled egg and smoked salmon tartlets

Add a touch of sophistication to brunch by serving these elegant tartlets instead of scrambled eggs on toast.
For a truly creamy result it is vital not to overcook the eggs.

Preparation time **20 minutes**
Total cooking time **20 minutes**
Makes 6

¹/2 quantity short pastry
  (see page 58)
6 sprigs fresh chervil, to garnish

FILLING
1 tablespoon unsalted butter
6 eggs
¹/3 cup heavy cream
¹/4 lb. smoked salmon, cut into thin strips
2 teaspoons caviar or lumpfish roe, to garnish

1 Preheat the oven to 400°F. Grease six 2³/4 x ⁵/8-inch fluted tartlet pans. Roll out the pastry on a lightly floured surface to a circle approximately ¹/8-inch thick. Cut out six circles with a 5-inch plain round pastry cutter, and use them to line the prepared pans (see Chef's techniques, page 59).

2 Bake blind for about 7 minutes, or until firm. Remove the weights and paper, and bake for another 3–5 minutes, or until the center is golden (see Chef's techniques, page 59). Remove the tartlets from the pans and keep warm.

3 To make the filling, heat the butter in a skillet over low to medium heat. Whisk the eggs lightly with the cream, and pour into the pan. Cook the eggs, over low heat, stirring with a wooden spoon to scrape the egg from the base of the pan, until just setting but still very creamy in consistency. Remove from the heat and stir in half the smoked salmon until well combined.

4 Fill the warm pastry tartlets immediately with the egg mixture. Decorate each with the remaining smoked salmon and a little caviar, and garnish with a small sprig of chervil. Serve warm.

Chef's tip Always remove the pan from the heat while the scrambled eggs are just creamy. The pan is hot and the eggs will continue to cook as you serve them. When overcooked, the eggs will be tough and water will begin to run from them.

Chèvre and watercress quiche

The rather peppery flavor of the watercress complements the creamy goat cheese filling in this recipe. This quiche could also be made as individual tartlets and served either warm or cold.

Preparation time **30 minutes**
Total cooking time **1 hour 15 minutes**
Serves **4–6**

FILLING
1/2 lb. watercress
3 eggs
1/3 cup heavy cream
nutmeg, to taste
5 oz. chèvre (goat cheese), cut into
   5/8-inch slices

1/2 quantity short pastry
   (see page 58)
1 egg, beaten

1 To make the filling, remove the large stems from the watercress, rinse and pat dry with paper towels. Bring 2 quarts water to a boil, add some salt and cook the watercress for 10 seconds. Drain, refresh in iced water for 3 minutes, then drain again (see Chef's techniques, page 63). Squeeze out any excess water, then coarsely chop the watercress. Season with salt and pepper.

2 Preheat the oven to 350°F. Lightly grease an 81/4 x 1-inch fluted tart pan with removable base. Roll out the dough on a lightly floured surface to a thickness of 1/8 inch and line the prepared pan (see Chef's techniques, page 59). Bake blind for about 25 minutes, or until firm. Remove the weights and paper, and brush the bottom of the pastry with the beaten egg. Bake for another 7 minutes (see Chef's techniques, page 59).

3 Whisk the eggs with the cream, and season with nutmeg, salt and pepper. Sprinkle the bottom of the shell with the chopped watercress, and arrange the slices of chèvre on top. Add the egg mixture and bake for 30–40 minutes, or until set and a knife inserted into the center comes out clean. Place on a wire rack to cool slightly before removing from the pan. Allow to stand for 5 minutes before cutting.

Anchovy sticks

Anchovy sticks, with light crisp pastry and salty anchovies, are delicious served with wine and champagne, hence their popularity at cocktail parties.

Preparation time **20 minutes + 30 minutes chilling**
Total cooking time **10 minutes**
Makes about 80

¹/2 quantity puff pastry (see page 60)
 or 8 oz. puff pastry trimmings
1 egg, beaten
20–25 anchovy fillets

1 Lightly dust a 17 x 12-inch baking sheet (quarter sheet pan) with flour. Roll out the puff pastry on a lightly floured surface to a rectangle the approximate size of the baking sheet. The pastry should be rolled out as thinly as possible—thin enough to read through. Carefully lift the puff pastry onto the baking sheet, then cover with plastic wrap and refrigerate for 20 minutes.

2 Preheat the oven to 400°F. Cut the pastry in half lengthwise and carefully transfer to a lightly floured work surface. Brush one of the strips with some beaten egg. Lay the anchovy fillets across the egg-brushed pastry at approximately 1-inch intervals. Lay the remaining strip of pastry over the top and roll lightly with the rolling pin to press the layers together. Cut the pastry lengthwise, at ¹/2-inch intervals, to make long strips, then cut across the strips to make sticks about 2³/4 inches long. Refrigerate for 10 minutes.

3 Place the anchovy sticks on two lightly greased baking sheets, and brush with the beaten egg. Bake for about 8–10 minutes, or until they are puffed and golden brown. Serve either warm or cold.

Chef's tip If you don't like your anchovies too salty, soak them in cool water for about 30 minutes, then pat dry.

Leek and Brie flamiche

The flamiche derives its name from the Flemish word for cake, as originally it was in fact a type of cake made from bread dough and served with butter. Nowadays, however, it usually refers to a pie filled with vegetables or cheese, or both, as in this particular recipe.

*Preparation time **1 hour 5 minutes**
+ **30 minutes chilling***
*Total cooking time **55 minutes***
Serves 4–6

PASTRY
2 cups all-purpose flour
I teaspoon salt
1/4 cup unsalted butter
I egg
I egg yolk

I egg, beaten

FILLING
1/4 cup unsalted butter, cubed
**3 1/2 cups leeks, white part only, thinly sliced
   (see page 63)**
5 oz. Brie
I egg
I egg yolk
3 tablespoons heavy cream

1 To make the pastry, sift the flour and salt together into a bowl. Using your fingertips, rub in the butter until the mixture resembles fine bread crumbs. Make a well in the center and add the egg, egg yolk and 3 tablespoons water. Mix well, shape into a ball and refrigerate for 20 minutes, wrapped in plastic wrap.

2 To make the filling, melt the butter in a deep skillet and slowly cook the leeks, covered, for 5 minutes. Cook for another 5 minutes, uncovered, or until all the liquid has evaporated, being careful not to allow the leeks to brown. Transfer the leeks to a strainer and set aside to allow to cool.

3 Preheat the oven to 325°F. Lightly grease an 8 1/4 x 1-inch fluted tart pan with removable base. Divide the pastry in half and roll out one half on a lightly floured surface to a thickness of 1/8 inch and line the prepared pan (see Chef's techniques, page 59), leaving a 1/2-inch overhang. Roll out the second piece of dough on a lightly floured surface to an 8 3/4-inch circle, and refrigerate until needed.

4 Remove the rind of the cheese and cut the cheese into small cubes. Spread the leeks over the bottom of the pastry shell, and sprinkle with the cheese. Whisk together the egg, egg yolk and cream. Pour over the leeks and cheese. Brush the edge of the pastry with the beaten egg and place the second piece of pastry on top. Trim the top pastry sheet so that it is even with the lower sheet. Pinch the dough well to seal the two pieces together, and trim the edges by pressing down with the thumb against the fluted edge of the pan. Brush the top with the egg and refrigerate for 10 minutes. Brush again with the beaten egg and cut a hole in the center using a small round cutter. Bake for 40–45 minutes, or until golden. Place on a wire rack to cool slightly before removing from the pan. Allow to stand for 5 minutes before cutting.

Asparagus feuilletés with chive butter sauce

Feuilletés are puff pastry cases that are generally filled with meat, vegetables or seafood.
They can be either square, rectangular, triangular or diamond-shaped. In this recipe they are filled
with asparagus and Brie, and served with a mouthwatering chive butter sauce.

Preparation time **20 minutes + 20 minutes chilling**
Total cooking time **25 minutes**
Makes 8

FILLING
16 fresh asparagus tips, about
 2¹/₂ inches long
3 oz. Brie, cut into 8 slices

¹/₂ quantity puff pastry (see page 60)
I egg, beaten

CHIVE BUTTER SAUCE
²/₃ cup unsalted butter, chilled and cubed
I teaspoon lemon juice
2 tablespoons chopped fresh chives

1 To make the filling, bring a pan of salted water to a boil, add the asparagus tips and cook for 2–3 minutes, or until tender. Drain the asparagus, refresh in iced water for 5 minutes, drain again, then transfer to a plate to cool (see Chef's techniques, page 63).
2 Roll out the pastry on a lightly floured surface to a 10¹/₂ x 8¹/₂-inch rectangle, approximately ¹/₄-inch thick. Trim the two long sides to straighten them, and cut the pastry into eight 2³/₄-inch diamonds or squares. Place slightly apart on a damp baking sheet and refrigerate for 20 minutes.

3 Preheat the oven to 400°F. Brush the top surface of the pastry with beaten egg. Do not brush the side edges as the egg will set and prevent the pastry from rising. Lightly score the top of the pastry in a crisscross pattern with a thin knife. Bake for approximately 15 minutes, or until well risen, crisp and golden brown. Split in half horizontally with a sharp knife, and scrape out any soft dough. Place a slice of Brie in the pastry cases and top with the asparagus so that the tips are just protruding. Replace the pastry lid and keep warm in a 300°F oven.
4 To make the sauce, bring ¹/₃ cup water to a boil in a saucepan. Reduce the heat and whisk in the butter, a few pieces at a time, until the butter is well incorporated and the sauce is thickened. Season with salt and pepper, and stir in the lemon juice and chives.
5 To serve, spoon a little of the chive sauce into each pastry case and drizzle some of the sauce onto the plate. Serve warm.

Chef's tip Any leftover puff pastry can be used to make anchovy sticks (see page 49).

Seafood quiche

The filling for this lovely seafood quiche is extemely quick and simple to prepare
when the seafood is purchased precooked.

Preparation time 35 minutes
Total cooking time 1 hour 10 minutes
Serves 4–6

1/2 quantity short pastry (see page 58)
I egg, beaten

FILLING
6 oz. cooked shelled small shrimp
6 oz. cooked crabmeat
3 eggs
I cup heavy cream
nutmeg, to taste
1/3 cup shredded Gruyère cheese

1   Preheat the oven to 325°F. Lightly grease an 8³/4 x
1¹/4-inch fluted tart pan with removable base. Roll out

the pastry on a lightly floured surface to a thickness of
1/8 inch and line the prepared pan (see Chef's
techniques, page 59). Bake blind for about 25 minutes,
or until firm. Remove the weights and paper, and brush
the bottom of the pastry with the beaten egg. Bake for
another 3 minutes (see Chef's techniques, page 59).

2   To make the filling, drain any excess water or juice
from the seafood and place on paper towels. Whisk the
eggs, cream and nutmeg together. Season with salt and
freshly ground pepper.

3   Sprinkle the seafood over the bottom of the pastry
shell. Pour in the egg mixture, sprinkle with the
shredded cheese and bake for 35–40 minutes, or until
the top is golden brown and a knife inserted into the
center comes out clean. Set on a wire rack to cool
slightly before removing from the pan. Allow to stand
for 5 minutes before cutting. Serve warm, accompanied
by a crisp green salad.

Ham gougères

Traditionally a gougère is a round or ring-shaped cheese cream-puff pastry. This variation uses plain choux pastry and a sprinkling of cheese to make small puffs that are then filled with a creamy smoked ham and cheese sauce.

Preparation time **30 minutes**
Total cooking time **25 minutes**
Serves 6

1 quantity cream-puff pastry
 (see page 62)
1 egg, beaten with a pinch of salt
1 tablespoon grated Gruyère or Parmesan cheese

FILLING
2 tablespoons unsalted butter
1/4 cup all-purpose flour
1 cup milk
1/3 cup finely shredded Gruyère cheese
2/3 cup finely diced smoked ham
1 teaspoon prepared English mustard
pinch of cayenne pepper
pinch of white pepper

1 Grease a baking sheet and refrigerate until needed. Preheat the oven to 400°F. Spoon the pastry into a pastry bag fitted with a 1/2-inch plain nozzle. Pipe 12 rounds of pastry onto the prepared baking sheet, approximately 1/2 inch at the base and 5/8 inch high. Brush the pastry with the beaten egg, and sprinkle with the shredded cheese. Bake for about 20 minutes, or until golden brown all over. Once baked, allow the cream-puffs to cool in the oven with the heat turned off and the oven door open. This will help dry out the inside of the pastry.

2 To make the filling, melt the butter in a heavy-bottomed saucepan over low to medium heat. Sprinkle the flour over the base of the pan and cook for 1–2 minutes without browning, stirring constantly with a wooden spoon. Slowly add the milk to the flour mixture, whisking vigorously to prevent lumps forming. Bring to a boil over medium heat, then simmer for 3–4 minutes. If the sauce has lumps, pass it through a fine strainer and reheat in a clean saucepan. Stir in the cheese, ham and mustard. Season to taste with salt, cayenne and white pepper.

3 Spoon the filling into a pastry bag fitted with a small round nozzle. Using the tip of a small knife, make a hole in the bottom of each pastry puff. Place the tip of the pastry bag into the hole and fill with the cheese mixture. Repeat with all the puffs. Serve warm with a salad, allowing two per person.

Chef's techniques

◆

Short pastry

This delicious dough produces one of the most versatile pastries for quiches and tarts, and is also one of the easiest to make.

*Preparation time **10 minutes + 20 minutes chilling***
*Total cooking time **None***
Makes about 1 lb. (2 tart shells)

1²/3 cups all-purpose flour
large pinch of salt
¹/3 cup unsalted butter, chilled
1 egg, lightly beaten
2–3 teaspoons water

1 In a large bowl, sift together the flour and salt. Cut the butter into small 1/2-inch cubes and place in the flour.
2 Rub the butter into the flour using your fingertips until the mixture resembles fine bread crumbs.
3 Make a well in the center and pour in the combined egg and water.
4 Slowly work the mixture together with a palette knife or pastry scraper until it makes a rough ball. If it is slightly sticky, add a little more flour. Turn out onto a lightly floured cool surface and knead very gently until just smooth (no more than 20 seconds). Wrap the pastry in plastic wrap and chill for at least 20 minutes before using.

Chef's tip This quantity of pastry is enough to line two shallow 7–8-inch tart pans. If only making one tart, divide the pastry into two pieces and wrap separately in plastic wrap. Use one piece and put the second one in a plastic bag and seal airtight, to freeze and use another time.

Put the cubes of butter in the flour and salt, and rub into the dry ingredients.

Continue rubbing the butter into the flour until the mixture resembles fine bread crumbs.

Pour the combined egg and water into the well.

Slowly work the mixture together with a palette knife until it makes a rough ball.

Lining a tart pan

Be very careful when handling the dough to avoid stretching it.

Place the dough over a rolling pin and unroll loosely over the pan.

Press the sides of the pastry into the flutes or sides of the pan by using a small ball of excess pastry.

Use a rolling pin to trim the pastry edges. Gently but firmly roll across the top of the pan. Refrigerate for 10 minutes.

Pierce the pastry shell with a fork to allow steam to escape during baking.

Baking blind

Baking the pastry before adding the filling prevents the base becoming soggy during cooking.

Crush a sheet of waxed paper lightly into a ball. Open out the paper, then lay it inside the pastry shell.

Spread a layer of pie weights or rice over the paper, then press down gently so that the weights or rice and the paper rest firmly against the sides of the shell.

Bake according to the time specified in the recipe, or until firm. Remove the weights or rice and paper.

If indicated in the recipe, rebake until the pastry looks dry and is evenly colored.

Puff pastry

This pastry requires more effort and time than the other pastries, but the result is a lovely buttery and flaky base for any tart or pastry. If you are short of time, purchased sheets of frozen puff pastry can be used.

Preparation time **1 day**
Total cooking time **None**
Makes about 1 lb.

DOUGH BASE
2 cups bread or all-purpose flour
I teaspoon salt
2–3 drops of lemon juice
¹/2 cup water
3 tablespoons unsalted butter, melted

¹/3 cup unsalted butter, chilled

1 To make the dough base, sift the flour and salt onto a cool work surface and make a well in the center. Add the lemon juice to the water, then place in the well with the butter and mix together with your fingertips. With the side of a palette knife or a pastry scraper, use a cutting action to gradually mix in the flour and work it into the butter mixture until the dry flour disappears and the mixture resembles loose crumbs. Bring together with your hands and knead lightly, adding a few drops of water if necessary, to make a smooth soft ball of dough.

2 Cut an "X" on top of the dough to prevent shrinkage, then wrap in lightly floured waxed paper or plastic wrap. Chill for 1 hour in the refrigerator—this will make the dough more pliable for rolling. Place the chilled butter between two pieces of waxed paper or plastic wrap. Tap it with the side of a rolling pin and shape into a 3/4-inch-thick square. This action will make the butter pliable to roll, without melting it.

3 Unwrap the dough and place it on a lightly floured cool surface. Roll the dough from just off center to form a cross shape with a mound in the center.

4 Place the butter on the central mound and fold over the four sides of the dough to enclose it completely.

Sift the flour and salt onto a work surface and make a well in the center. Add the lemon juice, water and butter and blend together with your fingertips.

Cut an "X" on top of the pastry with a sharp knife.

Unwrap the chilled dough and place it on a lightly floured surface. Roll from just off center to form a cross shape with a mound in the center.

Place the butter on the central mound and fold over the four sides of the dough to enclose it.

5 Roll over the top and bottom of the dough to seal the edges. On a lightly floured surface, roll the dough into a 5 x 14-inch rectangle.

6 Fold in three by folding the bottom third up towards the middle and the top third down. Brush off the excess flour and make sure that the edges all meet neatly. Make an indentation with your finger to record the first roll and fold. Wrap in plastic wrap and chill for 30 minutes.

7 Give the dough a quarter turn with the folded side on your left as if it was a book. With a rolling pin, gently press down to seal the edges.

8 Repeat steps 5–7 three more times, remembering to record each roll with an indentation and chilling for 30 minutes after each roll. After two rolls and folds, you should have two indentations. The finished pastry should have four indentations, and will start to look smoother as you continue to roll and fold. Leave the dough to rest in the refrigerator for a final 30 minutes. The puff pastry is now ready to use. It can be frozen whole, or cut into smaller portions, then used as needed.

Chef's tips When making puff pastry, work on a cool surface to prevent the butter from melting and making a heavy dough. In hot weather, it may be necessary to refrigerate the dough for an extra 15 minutes during the final resting.

Making puff pastry is not difficult, but it is time consuming, so make two or three quantities at once and freeze the extra. Thaw the pastry by leaving it overnight in the refrigerator. Puff pastry will keep in the refrigerator for 4 days and in the freezer for 3 months.

Seal the edges of the dough by pressing down with a rolling pin. Roll the pastry into a rectangle.

Fold the dough in three by folding the bottom third up towards the middle and the top third down.

After chilling the dough, put it on the surface in front of you as before and turn it a quarter turn so that it looks like a book with the binding on the left. Press down to seal the edges, then roll, fold and chill again.

Continue rolling, folding and chilling, trying to maintain an even finish and neat corners.

Cream-puff pastry

This pastry dough is cooked twice to give the lightness found in éclairs and cream-puff pastry buns. Before the final baking, the paste is fairly wet and needs to be piped.

Preparation time **5 minutes**
Total cooking time **10–15 minutes**

¹/₂ cup all-purpose flour
¹/₂ cup water
3 tablespoons unsalted butter, cubed
pinch of salt
pinch of sugar
2 eggs

1 Sift the flour onto a sheet of waxed paper. Place the water, butter, salt and sugar in a saucepan. Heat until the butter and water come to a boil. Remove from the heat and add the flour all at once.
2 Mix well using a wooden spoon. Return to the heat and mix until a smooth ball forms and the paste leaves the sides of the pan.
3 Remove from the heat and place the paste in a bowl. Lightly beat the eggs in a small bowl. Using a wooden spoon or an electric mixer, add the eggs to the paste a little at a time, beating well after each addition.
4 The mixture is ready to use when it is smooth, thick and glossy.

Chef's tips It is essential when making cream-puff pastry to measure the ingredients carefully, because too much moisture can cause the cream-puff pastry to collapse. Traditionally, bakers weigh the eggs in order to determine the weight of the dry ingredients.

Don't be fooled by golden colored cream-puff pastry! If the cracks of the cream-puff pastry are still light yellow or much lighter than the rest of the cream-puff pastry, this indicates that the interior is not quite done. Reduce the temperature to 325°F and continue baking.

Once boiling, remove from the heat and immediately stir in the sifted flour.

Return the pan to the heat and cook until the mixture makes a smooth ball that comes away from the sides of the pan.

Remove from the heat and transfer the mixture to a bowl. Gradually beat in the eggs with a wooden spoon.

The mixture is ready to use when it is smooth, thick and glossy.

Broiling bell peppers

Broiling peppers allows you to remove their skins and produces a delicious sweet flavor.

Preheat a broiler. Cut the bell peppers in half and remove the seeds and membrane.

Broil the peppers until the skin blisters and blackens.
Place in a plastic bag and allow to cool. When cool, peel off the skin.

Refreshing vegetables

The process of refreshing helps retain the vibrant color of blanched vegetables.

Cook the vegetables in boiling water until tender.

Drain, and plunge into a bowl of iced water to stop the cooking process and refresh the vegetables. Drain.

Preparing tomatoes

Many recipes call for peeled, seeded tomatoes. It is an easy process if you follow these instructions.

Using a very sharp knife, score a small cross in the base of each tomato.

Blanch the tomatoes in a large pan of boiling water for 10 seconds. Remove and plunge into a bowl of ice-cold water to stop the cooking and keep the flesh firm.

Pull away the skin from the cross, and discard the skins. If a recipe calls for the removal of the tomato seeds, cut the tomato in half and use a teaspoon to gently scoop out the seeds.

Washing leeks

Leeks are often used in cooking because they impart a unique flavor.

Before use, leeks need to be rinsed thoroughly under cold running water to dislodge and remove all traces of dirt or grit. Slit the green tops to help the water run through the tightly furled leaves.

First published in the United States in 1998 by Periplus Editions (HK) Ltd., with editorial offices at
153 Milk Street, Boston, Massachusetts 02109.

Murdoch Books and Le Cordon Bleu thank the 32 masterchefs of all the Le Cordon Bleu Schools, whose knowledge and
expertise have made this book possible, especially: Chef Cliche (MOF), Chef Terrien, Chef Boucheret, Chef Duchêne (MOF),
Chef Guillut, Chef Steneck, Paris; Chef Males, Chef Walsh, Chef Hardy, London; Chef Chantefort, Chef Bertin, Chef Jambert,
Chef Honda, Tokyo; Chef Salembien, Chef Boutin, Chef Harris, Sydney; Chef Lawes, Adelaide; Chef Guiet, Chef Denis, Ottawa.
Of the many students who helped the Chefs test each recipe, a special mention to graduates David Welch and Allen Wertheim.
A very special acknowledgment to Directors Susan Eckstein, Great Britain, and Kathy Shaw, Paris, who have been responsible for
the coordination of the Le Cordon Bleu team throughout this series.

The Publisher and Le Cordon Bleu also wish to thank Carole Sweetnam for her help with this series.

First published in Australia in 1998 by Murdoch Books®

Managing Editor: Kay Halsey
Series Concept, Design and Art Direction: Juliet Cohen
Editor: Justine Upex
Food Director: Jody Vassallo
Food Editors: Roslyn Anderson, Tracy Rutherford
US Editor: Linda Venturoni Wilson
Designer: Norman Baptista
Photographers: Damian Webber, Chris Jones
Food Stylists: Marie-Hélène Clauzon, Mary Harris
Food Preparation: Christine Sheppard, Michelle Earl, Kerrie Mullins
Chef's Techniques Photographer: Reg Morrison
Home Economists: Michelle Lawton, Kerrie Mullins, Justine Poole, Kerrie Ray

Library of Congress catalog card number: 98-85724
ISBN 962-593-448-0

Front cover: Spinach and ricotta quiche

Distributed in the United States by
Charles E. Tuttle Co., Inc.
RR1 Box 231-5
North Clarendon, VT 05759
Tel: (802) 773-8930
Fax: (802) 773-6993

PRINTED IN SINGAPORE

05 04 03 02 01 00 99 98   10 9 8 7 6 5 4 3 2 1

Important: Some of the recipes in this book may include raw eggs, which can cause salmonella poisoning.
Those who might be at risk from this (the elderly, pregnant women, young children and those suffering
from immune deficiency diseases) should check with their physicians before eating raw eggs.